# THE PERSONAL ENTREPRENEUR: HOW TO EXPLODE YOUR INCOME WITH ONLYFANS

## *THE COMPLETE GUIDE ON HOW TO START, SETUP, AND GROW YOUR ONLYFANS BUSINESS*

By

*CAROLYN FISHER*

# TABLE OF CONTENTS

## Legal Notes

The Personal Entrepreneur: How to Explode Your Income With OnlyFans is meant for entertainment and educational use only. All attempts have been made to present factual information in an unbiased context. The producer of this book is not an accountant or attorney, please make sure to consult with professionals regarding the creation of any business opportunity.

# WHY ONLYFANS

Social media has become an increasingly lucrative space for many influencers and social media personalities over the last several years. If you've picked up this book, you may be exploring your own options as a social media presence or may have already established a name for yourself in your space.

While there are opportunities out there, some of you may not always have the freedom you need to share what you want with your fans via social media. You may have many fans and those fans may all be loyal, but you don't always have a clear way to turn that loyalty into revenue for your brand. The space you work in or the nature of your work, too, can sometimes prevent you from accessing some of the marketing partnerships other influencers are able to leverage as revenue-driving opportunities. Social media sites such as Instagram, Facebook, or Twitter often shadow ban or ban outright users such as you trying to reach out to fans.

That's where OnlyFans steps in. Whatever your role is online and as an influencer, at the end of the day, you are one thing— a businessperson. In this book, you'll learn how to monetize your online presence through OnlyFans and drive up the revenue your brand already generates on social media. This innovative platform lets content creators just like you transform their existing fan base into a revenue stream via direct funding, tips, and additional features such as Pay-Per-View.

OnlyFans has an audience of at least 12 million users. It is primarily an adult entertainment site, but it also features some physical fitness influencers who want more freedom in how they promote their brand. The content is completely unrestricted, meaning anything and almost everything goes! What this means for you as an online presence is that you can build your brand free from censure or judgment.

It also means that you can monetize your presence. Your fans subscribe and you receive 80 percent of that revenue. OnlyFans gets 20 percent. The benefits you get from establishing an OnlyFans presence outweigh this fee. For one, the design of OnlyFans takes away any of the headaches you may have experienced in the past when it comes to monetizing your work and receiving payment. It is also much easier than designing and setting up your own site. Finally, since it is social media, it adds value to your brand by encouraging community amongst your fans, which, in turn, can build brand loyalty for you.

OnlyFans is the next, great social media space and an ideal opportunity for you if your brand has been held back by content restrictions on other social media platforms. This ebook will walk you through everything you need to know to create and leverage an OnlyFans profile.

# SETTING UP A PROFILE

First off, let's be clear— you have to be 18 to set up a profile on OnlyFans. While there are a wide variety of personalities on the site, much of the content is adult. So, if you set up an account, please only do so if you are over the age of 18.

Before we dive into the details of setting up your account and profile, let's take a moment to walk through an overview of what a standard profile looks like. This will help you understand everything that is to come as you set up your profile.

## PROFILE DETAILS

Each profile has a structure similar to what you might see on any other social media site. A banner image or "cover" image runs across the top of the page, with a profile picture below it to the left. At the top of a profile, you will also see a series of tabs:

- A Posts tab that takes you to the user's posts
- A Photos tab that takes you to the user's photos
- A Videos tab that links you to their videos; and,
- A Likes tab that shows the total number of fans a user has.

If you go to an OnlyFans profile and you are not a subscriber, you will see this:

This is the paywall. For you as a soon-to-be OnlyFans influencer, this is the component that allows you to monetize your brand on this site. Only fans who pay to subscribe to you can view any of your content.

Because of this setup, it is crucial that you take the first steps of the process of setting up your account seriously. These small choices are the hints you send out to new fans to convince them that they should subscribe to you on OnlyFans. Everything from username to a profile pic can convert a new fan, so choose carefully! These profile components will also help retain your existing fan base, showing your fans that you know what you're about and will continue to provide them with quality content.

With all that being said, let's dive into how you can set up your profile and get started making money on OnlyFans.

# Signing Up

To sign up and start the process on OnlyFan, you can do one of two things:

- Connect via your Twitter account
- Or sign up using an email account

You can sign up using either method, but connecting your account with Twitter comes with many advantages. It allows you to push content out to your followers directly, for one. It also lets you expand your OnlyFans fan base more readily via Tweets. Make the choice that is the right fit for you and your brand.

Once you use either format to log in, you should receive an email from OnlyFans asking you to verify your email. Click on the link in this email to verify your email and account. This will take you to a Profile detail page where you can set up essential data for your OnlyFans account, including:

- Your website URL
- An About blurb
- Your location, and

- An Amazon wishlist

We will look at each of these in detail further on in this guide.

You can also edit the names that you will be using on OnlyFans. Let's take a look at what this means.

# CHOOSING YOUR ONLYFANS NAMES

OnlyFans allows you to edit both the Username and the Display Name you will use on the site. Both of these are important branding and marketing tools you need to consider carefully.

The Username is the one that will be used to complete your personal URL on the site. For example, if your Username were [username], your fans could reach you by going to https://onlyfans.com/[username]. Since there may be some scenarios where you need to tell someone how to get to your OnlyFans profile rather than provide them with a direct link (such as in a video), you want this name to be something relatively easy to explain. Or, alternatively, you may already have a username established at the center of your brand; if so, make sure to use this one so that your fans can find you quickly and easily and so that you have cohesion across your online presence.

When you pick your Display Name, you need to think about your brand and what you are trying to accomplish on OnlyFans. Again, if you already have a name in your space, you will want to use that one. If you are creating one for the first time, you want it to stand out. You also want to make sure that it clearly represents your brand. If you are a fitness guru, for example, and your Display Name is something generic such as "gmd2019," no one is really going to understand what you're all about. Your Display Name should be something that speaks to your fans and the content you want to produce, and also draws people in. Make the Display Name clear, punchy, and reflective of who you are and what you're offering. You can use spaces to make it more legible and more appealing, too.

# CHOOSING YOUR COVER IMAGE AND PROFILE PHOTO

The next part of the process is maybe the single most essential component of your OnlyFans profile— your images. These images are the big draw, the special ingredient that pulls fans in and keeps your existing fans coming back. The online world is a hugely visual medium, and fans and users know a quality image when they see it. They will judge your brand in an instant if these images are not up to par and in keeping with some of the other influencers in your space.

One important note: These profile images cannot contain full nudity. These are the images that will get pushed out into the general online world via Twitter, other social media platforms, etc., and, as such, can't contain anything that would be deemed pornographic or inappropriate. How you will distinguish yourself in these images will have to come from your own creativity. Do some research and see what the heavy hitters in your space are doing. How are they presenting themselves in their profile images? Make sure that your images reflect the same tone, content, and quality.

Again, fans know these visuals well, and they will pass judgment on sub-par images. These images are what separate the big earners on OnlyFans from an average content creator. Remember the paywall we discussed a few sections back? If these images you choose for your profile and cover are not compelling, you will not convert new fans or encourage existing ones to commit to your OnlyFans profile through a subscription.

## COVER IMAGE

Your cover image is a banner image that stretches across the entire width of your profile on any screen. This image should relate to your content, but it can be more generic. Again, look around at other influencers in your space to determine the standard of the image being used in your niche.

Given the length and layout of a cover image, this is obviously a great opportunity to include some lounging body shots. Remember to keep it PG, as no nudity is allowed at this level of your profile.

Unsure of how to create a great cover image? There are professionals that can help out. One such option is

Fiverr, where you can find a professional photo editor who can help. This person can edit and season your image using Photoshop and other pro tools to get it up to the standards of your space. Your cover image will be the big draw, so make sure you have a killer image.

## PROFILE PHOTO

Your profile photo is just as important as your cover image, but it is more of a branding element than your cover image. Why? This is where fans get to see you or, more specifically, your face. The cover image is you in the abstract, your form. Your profile image is where you shine through. Share as much or as little as you want of your identity. Many OnlyFans influencers use masks or costumes to add mystique to their brands. Consider what works for you and create an image that reflects that. Remember, you want this image to pop off the page and make people click!

## THE ABOUT SECTION

Now let's circle back to setting up our About section. First off, you want to create some About content for your profile. This is the place where you add your bio or personal story.

This is paywall content, so no one will be able to see this until they subscribe to your profile. Once those fans are subscribed, however, this content will only add to your pull and mystique. Story is an important component of branding. You want to tell your story in a way that adds value to your brand and increases loyalty with your fan base.

Remember, users have shown some interest in you, which is why you got to this stage, so explain to them what they are going to get in return for subscribing. This little blurb can have a huge effect on your conversion rates. Make it easy to read but be detailed about what you will be delivering to your fans. Tell them what content you will share, what videos they will see; essentially, what they will be getting for their money. You will also want to let them know how often you will be posting. If you plan on offering custom content, let them know that in your About content as well.

## LOCATION

Location is an interesting one, sort of a double-edged sword. You want to provide some location detail to entice fans, but you don't want to provide *too* much. Location can excite and engage fans. If fans know you are a local or, alternatively, from a glamorous city, for example, this can make them more enthusiastic. You do, however, want to make sure you protect your privacy. Never reveal too much information here or elsewhere on your OnlyFans site that could allow a fan who is too dedicated to show up on your doorstep! Safety is important, so protect your interests here.

## Website URL

Some of you may have already been promoting yourself or monetizing your online brand via your own website. That's great, and you can include that information here. Insert your website URL in this section of your profile so that fans can click through. Make sure to also include a link on your site that links directly to your OnlyFans profile.

## AMAZON WISHLIST

This is a unique and great feature on OnlyFans. The Amazon Wishlist basically allows fans to give you presents! This links fans through to a wishlist associated with an Amazon account. They select an item on Amazon, purchase it, and then it gets sent to you. Easy! Be careful, however, to protect your security. You don't necessarily want this associated with your personal Amazon account and your personal information. Consider creating a separate Amazon account that you can use for business purposes to protect your privacy.

## Spotify Account

At the bottom of your profile setup, you will also see a link that allows you to link your Spotify account to your OnlyFans account. Linking your Spotify is a great way to enhance engagement. Your fans will be able to see what you're listening to and gain insights that keep them enticed and coming back. As with the Amazon Wishlist, you may want to link a generic business account, not your personal one.

# ADDING A BANK ACCOUNT

One of the reasons you are reading this book is so that you can find out how to monetize your online brand with OnlyFans. In order to do that, you need to add a bank account to your profile. This part of the process can trip up a lot of users. There are two stages involved:

1. You must submit your ID and personal details to OnlyFans so that they can confirm who you are.
2. After approval, you can add your bank info so that OnlyFans can transfer money to your account and so that you can set a subscription price for your profile

## GETTING APPROVAL

To get started on the approval process, click on the Add a Bank Account button from your Profile setup page. If you have not set up your images and your About info, you will not be able to start the approval process, so make sure to circle back and do that.

Once you are through to the bank info page, start entering your info, including your country name, address, and so on. You also have the option to add your Twitter or Instagram here, but that is not required.

You will also need to provide a government ID. Options that will work include a passport, an ID card, or a Driver's License. You will need to add a photo of your ID **and** a photo of you holding the ID. This is so that OnlyFans can confirm that you are, in fact, the owner of the bank account you are trying to add.

When you upload the ID images, make sure that the file size of the photo is not too big. At this part of the process, you will also need to declare whether or not you will be sharing explicit imagery on your OnlyFans profile. If you plan on doing that, select "Explicit Content" to confirm.

Once you have taken care of all this, just click on the button to send your info for approval to the OnlyFans team. The approval process will take around 48 hours, so don't worry if you don't hear back right away.

### ADDING A BANK ACCOUNT

Once you are approved by OnlyFans, you can add a bank account to start receiving payments and set your subscription prices. Click on the Profile icon on the right top of the page and select "Add Bank". The default method for delivering payments on OnlyFans is via Visa, but you do have other options. Other Payout options include Direct Transfers and International Bank Transfers. Direct Transfer is your fastest option, but it requires that you have earned at least $20 on your account. If you are transferring internationally, it will take longer. International transfers also require that you have $200 in your OnlyFans account.

When you've accomplished all this, you are ready to go! Now you can get started on actually using your OnlyFans site, posting images, sharing content, and getting your fans excited. Let's take a look.

# GETTING STARTED – HOW TO USE ONLYFANS AND ITS FEATURES

Now that you have your profile up and running and have set up your banking information so that you can start earning on OnlyFans, it's time to learn how to push content out to your fans, enhancing your base and deepening fan loyalty.

# POSTING TO YOUR FEED

There are two ways in which you can post to your feed. One way is to go to your profile and click on the "Create Post" button. A second and more direct way is to click on the plus icon on the header bar at the top of any page on OnlyFans.

Posting to your feed allows you to share messages, media, and even polls with your fans.

First, let's take a look at posts. Posts are typically little check-ins, updates, and messages you can send to your fans. As with any content that you push out on OnlyFans, you want it to be in keeping with your overall brand and messaging. Given the nature of much of the content on OnlyFans, you can also use this as a tease—an opportunity to entice your fans to keep subscribing or even pull in new fans. While unsubscribed fans can't see your images, they can see your post text. The right titillating words in tandem with your profile and cover photos can help pull in new subscriptions. Many OnlyFans influencers also use this as an opportunity to encourage tips, which we will look at in greater detail later on.

Once you have typed in your message, just click Post! It's that easy to start communicating with fans. This will post as a status update to your feed and appear on the feed of fans.

## ATTACHING MEDIA

When you create a post, you also have the option of attaching a photo or video. To do this, click on the Image icon at the bottom of the new post. You can attach either a photo or video. Be sure to include a text message that adds value to the image. Again, the more enticing, the better. You can also set up your images to encourage conversions, which we will look at in a bit.

Keep in mind that there are some data limits to what you can post. OnlyFans lets you post up to 20 pictures or one video in each post, and each image should be under 6000x6000 pixels. The video file size limit is 3GB, and the site supports only videos that are done in mp4, mov, avi, and mpeg4 video formats.

## ADDING A POLL

A unique feature of OnlyFans is that it gives you the ability to check in with your fans via polling. This gives you a way to know what is and what isn't working in your posts. It's also a great way to flirt with your fans and keep them interested. For example, you might post a poll asking fans what they want to see.

Use the responses to adjust your posts so that you can create the most compelling and engaging content for your fan base. You can set a duration for the poll as well. As you can see in the image above, we've set this poll to run for 7 days.

## SCHEDULING YOUR POST

Sometimes, you are busy and can't stay on top of your OnlyFans account as much as you like. One workaround is to schedule your posts in advance. Not only can you schedule the posts to post at a certain time, but you can also schedule several posts at once. In this way, you can get all your posting done for the week in one sitting, freeing up time to engage in other endeavors related to your business.

## ADDING A PRICE TO YOUR POST

Posts with media are the most important element of your profile on OnlyFans. Why? Because you can add a price to these posts. A simple text post will not let you do this. When you generate a post with media, add a price to your post, enticing fans to tip you and pay the price that you've set. You can do this in cute and coy ways. For example, the text of your post might read, "Tip me and I'll step out from behind this screen" or "Send me a tip and I'll take off this robe", and so on. Only media works with this, so brainstorm on how you can encourage fan dollars to come your way with the right images and text.

## GOING LIVE WITH SUBSCRIBERS

You also have the option of going live with subscribers, much like you would see an influencer on Instagram do. This is a great way to engage because it makes your fans feel like they are with you and really getting to know you. You can then take this video file and post it as a normal video at a later date, in case any of your loyal fans missed it.

## ADDING TO YOUR STORY

Adding to your Story on OnlyFans works similarly to Stories on Instagram and Facebook. A Story allows you to share a photo or video for a limited amount of time. You can then save the highlights for use at a later date.

# RECEIVING TIPS

Receiving tips is a major way you can supplement your income on OnlyFans. As mentioned earlier, you can monetize posts, encouraging fans to send you tips. The minimum you can charge for a tip is $5.00. Remember, the better the quality and quantity of your posts, the more likely you are to drive up sales via tips. Fans enjoy sending tips because it lets them feel as if they are interacting with you directly, so don't be shy about asking for them!

# Messages

As with other social media sites, OnlyFans offers users a messaging interface. Using messages on OnlyFans gives you two advantages:

- It lets you connect with other creators
- It lets you engage with fans through Pay Per View content

As with tips, the minimum you can ask for is $5.00 for paid message content. Again, this direct contact is really appealing for fans and makes them feel special.

In terms of communicating with other creators, reach out to people in your space. You will be surprised at how many will respond with tips and recommendations on how to excel on OnlyFans.

# SETTING A SUBSCRIPTION PRICE

Once you have added a Bank Account, you can set your subscription price for fans. To do this, click on your profile icon, then go to "My Profile" and click on "Edit Profile." You'll see the Subscription Price entry box right below your Display Name. The default is "Free," but you can set it for paid subscriptions. The minimum is $4.99/month. You might think that setting your price low will get you more subscriptions, but there are some techniques you can use to garner more subscriptions at a higher price point.

For example, try setting your subscription price at a higher price point— somewhere around $14.99. This higher premium makes you look like you are a higher profile creator, for one. What you can then do is offer a series of promotions, offering your subscription at a discounted rate. For example, you might post something along the lines of "Offering 50 percent off my subscription for just a few days. Don't miss out, or I'll miss you ☺", and so on. This adds a little pressure for fans to make a choice, but it also has the added advantage of making them feel as if they're getting a great deal.

That being said, the relationship between price and subscribers isn't absolute. The majority of the time, a lower price does lead to more subscribers. There are cases, however, where pricing yourself a bit higher can make fans feel as if they are getting a premium product, and this might make them more willing to pay more. Experiment and see what works for you. Whatever price you settle on, remember that OnlyFans will be taking 20 percent.

# Producing Content

Now that you know how to push out content, how do you start producing content that will compel your fan base to stay on as loyal subscribers? One way to start is by finding the right niche that works for you and your brand.

## Finding Your Niche

What is a niche? A niche is an area of the marketplace that's unique to people like you. It's also the place where your fans will go to look for people just like you.

A fashion blogger, for example, might exist in the larger space of "fashion." Her niche, however, might be Harajuku fashion for U.S. fans, for example.

Consider what your space is, then do your research. Look at other creators and influencers in your space and see what type of content they are generating. You can even consider subscribing to some of the more high-profile personalities in your space and see what type of content they are creating for fans.

Once you've done this research, start considering ways in which you are unique in your space. What differentiates you from others? By looking at this, you can start dialing in on your niche. The goal is not to appeal to everyone, but to appeal to a particular group that loves the very detailed and unique thing you are offering. By being yourself and playing to your unique strengths and distinct characteristics, you can start to build a following of truly loyal and committed fans.

## Interacting With Your Fans

Another way in which you can start producing the best content is by interacting with your fans. We already touched on how you can use polls to test the waters and see what your fan base wants. OnlyFans is unique in the world of social media in that it offers a lot of ways to interact with your fans directly. Not only can you poll to see where they are at with your content, but you can also communicate with them directly via messages. Send regular messages and maintain your network of connections. Monetizing your messages, too, can help you learn what is working and what isn't working with your fan base. Remember, the thrill of OnlyFans for your fans is that they get to be in direct contact with you, so take advantage of this feature!

## POSTING REGULARLY

The top creators and earners on OnlyFans have content coming out on the regular. This doesn't mean that they are always on OnlyFans posting content throughout the day. This means that they are just informed and savvy about how to post.

As we discussed earlier, you can batch your work and set up posts to post periodically throughout the week. We'll cover this in more detail later on in the Grow Your Audience section. For now, concentrate on one goal — keeping your feed popping up on your fan's timelines. This will keep them engaged and give you more opportunities for feedback that you can then use to perfect your content.

You also want to schedule a weekly time to go live. This needs to be consistent. Your fans rely on you, so not showing up when they expect you will dilute the essential loyalty that binds your fan base together. Your fans are arranging their schedules around when you go live, so be considerate by being consistent. Don't forget your polls— you can use these to figure out when the best times to go live are, ensuring that you get the most eyes on your content.

## STAYING WITH IT

As you begin expanding your profile and reach on OnlyFans, remember this— you need to stick with it. The majority of people who struggle to make money with OnlyFans fail because they don't stick with it long enough.

There is a long list of creators who stayed on OnlyFans for a week or two and then gave up when they didn't see results. You need to remain consistent and committed in the long term to see your business grow on OnlyFans. If you stay consistent, your following will grow and you will begin to see results.

# Different Ways to Make Money

Optimizing your content is your starting point. When your content is in a strong place and set up to attract fans, you can start diversifying the ways in which you make money on OnlyFans.

## Growing Subscriptions

One way to do this is to grow your subscription base. We've already discussed how you can entice fans with the right kind of posts and media. You now need to work at spreading the word across social media so that your OnlyFans content can be found.

Make sure that there is a link to your OnlyFans account anywhere you are online. This can be on Insta, Facebook, and your personal website. This funnels traffic that is already engaged by you toward your monetized content on OnlyFans.

On Instagram, make sure that the link is shared in your bio. Post regularly with Instagram approved images and reference your OnlyFans site, making sure to specify that the link is in your bio. On

Facebook, it's much easier. You can include links to your OnlyFans account directly in your status updates.

## Asking for Tips

The easiest way to get a tip? Ask! Tipping is a popular way for fans to show their appreciation, and you should never be ashamed to ask. You can do this through your posts or through your direct message interactions with fans. If you don't ask for tips, guess what? Chances are you won't get them. Fans are happy to do this for you because it enhances the sensation for them that they are engaging with you directly. As with any gift sent in your direction, make sure that you show your appreciation. Thanking fans who have tipped you makes them feel special, and it also has the added virtue of making other fans feel left out! They might just turn around and send you a tip so they can get their own special thanks.

## Custom Content

You can also sell customized content in exchange for tips. This can include a wide range of materials from photos and videos or customized PDF workout plans if you are a fitness influencer. Think creatively and find a way to generate customized content that is in keeping with your brand.

OnlyFans also lets you create a tip menu that shows the item and cost for these customized offerings. You should make sure that you pin this content to the top of your profile so that it's readily available to all your fans. Some of your fans might not even realize that this is an option if you don't promote your customized content in this way.

If you make a promise to deliver customized content to a fan, do it and do it on time. Nothing can dilute your brand's power more quickly than not holding up your end of the bargain. Make sure that you get the material to them quickly and that it is done well— you don't want to leave people waiting and risk not only losing a customer but also gaining some bad word of mouth.

# PayPerView Messages (PPV)

As we discussed earlier, you can send messages to your subscribers, which they must pay for in order to open them. These messages can include photos, audio, or video. The minimum you can charge for each one is $3, but price your PPV messages according to what the market can bear. Many of your loyal fans will be willing to pay more for certain content. You can create a price tier, too, explaining that some of the best content is only available at a higher price point.

If you want to promote PPV messages, you can send out a blanket message to all of your subscribers. As an alternative, consider reaching out to individual and particularly loyal or attentive fans. Do all of this via the Messages button. Your fans will receive a message with blurred out content but will not be able to see the detailed content. With the right message enticing them, you just might be able to drive some real conversions this way and up your revenue opportunities on OnlyFans.

# PRO TIPS FOR USING ONLYFANS

Now let's take a look at some tips you can leverage to start using OnlyFans like a pro and make the best use of your time.

First off, OnlyFans does not have an Android or iOS app at the moment. This means that you will not have direct and easy access to OnlyFans from your phone. To deal with this, create a shortcut to the OnlyFans site on the home screen of your phone. This way, you can get on the site quickly and respond to your fans in real time. Remember, leaving fans waiting will only dilute their engagement. A quick and friendly response will only deepen it.

If you use an Android phone, here's how you can create a link on your phone's home screen:

1. Open your Chrome browser and go to OnlyFans
2. Click on the Menu icon
3. Click "Add to Home Screen"

If you use an iPhone, do the following:

1. Open your Safari browser and go to OnlyFans

2. Click on the Share arrow
3. Pick "Add to Home Screen"

You will also want to make sure that your notifications in OnlyFans are set up to alert you to all activities on your account. To do this, go to your Settings page by clicking on Settings under your profile icon. Click on Notifications. You will see a list of items related to Notifications:

RECEIVE SITE NOTIFICATIONS ABOUT

- New Campaign Contribution
- New comment
- New Likes
- Discounts from users I used to follow
- New Subscriber
- New Tip

TOAST NOTIFICATIONS

- RECEIVE TOAST NOTIFICATIONS ABOUT
- New Campaign Contribution
- New comment
- New Likes
- New Subscriber

- New Tip

Toast notifications are pop-up notifications that you will receive on your computer. Site Notifications will appear on the OnlyFans site whenever you log in and will appear under the Bell icon at the top of the page. Make sure that all of these are selected so that you are alerted to any and all activities on your profile. You also want to make sure that Email Notifications are toggled to the "On" position, as well as Push Notifications. This is essential to ensure that you stay in touch with your fans, respond in a timely manner, and manage your account efficiently.

## Linking a Domain Name

Finally, another way to drive traffic to your OnlyFans profile is to link a domain name directly to your OnlyFans account. Go to GoDaddy or another vendor of domain names and see if there is a domain available that relates to your profile and brand. You will need to purchase this domain name, which should be relatively affordable. Once you have this domain name purchased, make sure that it links directly to your account so that fans, old and new alike, can find you quickly and easily.

# Growing Your Audience

The biggest part of having success on OnlyFans is developing a strong fan base. Let's take a moment now to consider how you can do this.

First off, a strong fan base doesn't have to be enormous. Consider this: If you are able to grow and retain 1000 fans, this will translate into $3000 a month in revenue. That's a pretty sizeable return on your investment. Unlike other social media platforms such as Instagram, OnlyFans allows you to generate income with a smaller fan base. On Instagram, influencers need to have followers in the tens of thousands before they can start seeing any ROI.

Those other social media sites can be helpful, however. They can be key elements in growing your fan base on OnlyFans. If you grow your social media followers and make sure that all of your social media profiles link to your OnlyFans profile, you will begin to see that your OnlyFans fan base will grow on its own.

You have one goal in promoting your OnlyFans profile via your other social media profiles: Getting 3 to 5 percent of your followers on other sites to become subscribers on OnlyFans.

When you think of it that way, it's far less intimidating.

How do you grow your social media fan base and drive this 5 percent toward your OnlyFans profile? There are a number of ways. Whatever you do, however, you need to keep certain things in mind:

1. **Do not post explicit images on other social media sites.** This is a surefire way to get your account wiped. What's more, you will lose all of the followers you have on that social media site in one fell swoop. Make sure that you are **always** posting in adherence to that site's Terms of Use.

2. **Posting within the Terms of Use doesn't mean you have to be buttoned up.** Plenty of social media users push the boundaries. Do a little research on what leaders in your space are sharing. Chances are they are pushing boundaries without violating the Terms of Use. There are ways to do it, so learn from the experts.

Growing your fan base is a self-fulfilling prophecy in many ways. This is because a larger number of fans means that new fans will be that much more impressed and much more likely to subscribe. In other words, increasing your numbers increases your numbers!

# CREATING A CONTENT PLAN

You are running a business, and any business has to create a content plan to promote and market itself online. Just because your business is personal and based on personal connection does not mean you shouldn't approach it in a professional and systematic way.

You want to post content and post it consistently. Create a plan and batch-produce your content as we discussed earlier. You also want to develop a monthly calendar that you can adhere to.

In order to meet this schedule, block out two days each week during which you will develop content. Again, your content has to be of the highest quality. Given the digital age, it can be quite easy to take great pictures, for example, but not all of us are adept at doing this.

If you don't feel as if your photos and videos are up to par, consider working with a professional. Student photographers and filmmakers can be a good way to get good content at a lower price point if you are concerned about costs. The return you will get in new subscriptions from high-grade content, however, will be worth the initial investment.

If you are not the best writer, you can also consider working with a contractor to generate your posts. There are a wide number of freelancers out there on places such as Fiverr and Upwork who can help you post and even market yourself across social media.

Once you have the content of your posts in hand, set a posting schedule around peak times so that you get the most eyes on each post. As we discussed earlier, peak times can vary from niche to niche. Do your research and follow the posts of some of the most successful creators in your space. This will show you when the peak times are so that you can build your posting schedule around this.

You can also experiment with posting times yourself. Set a schedule for one week and see how it works, then make tweaks for week two. In this way, you will be able to see whether or not certain times of the day are really best for you and your brand or not.

# CROSS PROMOTION

Another way to grow your fan base is to work with other OnlyFans creators via cross promotion. Cross promotion involves either both of you promoting one another in your niche or the other party promoting you in return for something else.

Cross promotion with your peers on OnlyFans has a number of benefits, including:

- It provides you access to more followers who are already on OnlyFans and are familiar with the platform.
- It gives you access to fans who have demonstrated that they are willing to pay for a subscription.
- It gives you access to a "warm audience", or one that is already acclimated to your space and your type of message.

There are two ways in which you can approach cross promotion with other content creators on OnlyFans. One is called Peer Cross Promotion and the other is called Level Up Cross Promotion.

## THE PEER MODEL OF CROSS PROMOTION

The Peer model of cross promotion involves reaching out to creators who have a similar following to you. They are in the same niche and they have the same number of followers. These content creators are just what the name tells you— your peers.

Do some research in your niche to find several options that qualify as your peers in your space. Next, reach out to them, offering to set up a cross promotion deal with them. What this means is that you will promote them and they will promote you. This is a win-win scenario for both of you, as you will both be able to grow your fans and subscribers.

You will need to reach out to several individuals, as not everyone will be ready to make a deal. Some of them may already have cross promotion deals set up while others may just not be up for it! Getting in touch with several people increases your chances of finding someone who is ready and willing to work with you.

## THE LEVEL UP MODEL OF CROSS PROMOTION

The Level Up model is something a bit different. In this approach, you reach out to people in your niche who are a bit *more* successful than you. They have bigger fan bases, more subscribers, and are likely making more money.

That being said, why would they want to cross-promote with you? Well, you will likely need to offer them something in return. Ask them how you can get their help. Say that you are looking to level up and can benefit from their help and guidance. Many times, they will ask that you pay them a fee. This is fine, and it is par for the course. As with an investment in a professional photographer or online marketing maven, working with this professional will give you a sizeable return on your investment. The revenue you will generate from the new fans this deal delivers will more than make up for the initial fee.

In some cases, the Level Up creator may be willing to help you for free. If you build a connection with them and they see something of themselves in you, they just may be willing to help you out. Work on building a connection and relationship and see what happens!

# How to Keep Your Subscribers

Once you've done all this legwork, chances are that you've been able to increase the number of subscribers you have on OnlyFans. Great! Now, how do you keep them?

Yes, you need to try to retain your subscribers. Many fans can lose interest, get distracted, or bail after the first month. Work proactively to stop this from happening.

First off, you need to be consistent, as we stated earlier. Follow up on all your promises. When you say a new post is coming, share that post. When you agree to provide customized content, create and deliver that content on time.

More importantly, stay in touch with your fan base. Regular posts are a start, but you can also communicate directly with them via messages. As any salesperson will tell you, it's easier to keep existing contracts than generate new ones. So, work hard at letting your fans know that you care about them and want them to stick around in the long term.

One big pro tip? Creating the buildup. You don't want each of your posts to be a one-off or independent post that has nothing to do with any other post. Take some time to build up to big posts and keep your audience engaged. You can do this by hinting at what's to come in some early posts, then delivering big after a few days or a week. Whatever schedule you promise, stick to it! The anticipation and the final delivery will excite your fans and keep them coming back for more.

You also want to welcome fans when they are new subscribers. This simple act of welcome will make them feel special, and it is a critical first step in your ongoing engagement with a fan. The first moment they subscribe is your golden opportunity to capture them and turn them into lifelong fans.

What's even better about this approach? OnlyFans allows you to set this up so that it goes out automatically every time someone subscribes:

1. Go to your setting then click on Chats.
2. Look for "Welcome For New Fans" and click the gray button to turn it blue and activate it.

3. Create a custom message that is going to speak directly to your new subscribers.
4. Welcome them and give them specifics, letting them know about your posting schedule and about the different parts of your profile they can explore.
5. Most importantly... THANK THEM!

An enticing add-on that a lot of professional creators on OnlyFans use is including a question in the welcome message. You could also ask them a question and encourage them to send you a message. In this way, you start the process of engagement and develop that connection that will keep them on as subscribers.

## CREATING A PROMO VIDEO

Another way to keep fans on the hook and coming back for more is to create a promo video. You can only do this once you have been working on OnlyFans for a while and have accumulated a good deal of quality content, but it is well worth the wait. Once you have been working for a little bit, create a promo video of your best content that will be displayed on your profile and will encourage new fans to subscribe. You can pin it to the top of your feed so that everyone can see it. This promo will also keep existing fans engaged, reminding them of favorite posts from the past.

Already have something else pinned to the top? Don't worry. You can just upload your promo video as a story and then save the story as a highlight that will always stay on the top of your profile.

## CREATING AN FAQ

As your fan base continues to grow and you gain more experience on OnlyFans, you will likely receive a lot of questions from fans. Some will be about your content; others will be personal to you and your brand. Once you have compiled a number of questions, create a FAQ page for your fans. This will give them a quick and easy way to find answers, but it also can help engage new fans, as it gives them more detail about you and how you work. You can also use your FAQs as an opportunity to pose questions to your fans that can continue and expand on your engagement.

# PROMOTING YOUR ACCOUNT

In conclusion, let's walk through some techniques you can use on OnlyFans to promote your account.

One is to run discounted subscription prices. We touched on this earlier when we looked at how much you should charge for subscriptions. Running promotions is a great way to pull in new fans. You can also set your promotions to expire at a certain time or after a certain number of subscribers. This is advantageous because you can set a goal and meet it without running the risk of too many taking advantage of the discount.

A promotion is also a good way to pull in fans who may have been on the fence about subscribing to you. Maybe money is a concern for them, or maybe they just weren't that engaged and weren't willing to pay a certain price point. Seeing the lower rate may well be the extra push they need to commit.

Also, consider turning to Snapchat. This quick and engaging platform is a reliable way to pull in more fans and followers. The rapid-fire nature of Snapchat also lends itself to flirty and enticing posts that engage fans like yours.

Finally, find influencers on Snapchat in a field similar to yours and ask them for advice via messages. The best way to vet an influencer is to ask them to send you a screenshot of their insights. This does a few things:

- It ensures that they have a large audience (Snapchat will only give insights to people with a large audience).

- It allows you to see how many views they get and how many people are watching.

- You get a breakdown of the demographics of their fan base, including sex, age group, etc.

These data points will give you enormous insight into what works on Snapchat. You want to find one that has had at least a million views in the last month. Remember:

**More views=more clicks=more chances for subscribers**

The average online conversion rate is somewhere between 2-3%, so you will need to build up your volume of clicks.

## Conclusion

You've absorbed a lot of information here, and it will hopefully put you in good stead to start charting your own course on OnlyFans. This platform provides enormous advantages to many who have been working in niches that other social media platforms do not cater to or allow to flourish.

Take the knowledge you've gained here and access all the opportunities OnlyFans has to offer. With the right level of commitment and high-quality work, you can turn your OnlyFans profile into the revenue generator you've always wanted.

www.ingramcontent.com/pod-product-compliance
Lightning Source LLC
Chambersburg PA
CBHW020614220526
45463CB00006B/2588